COPING WITH . . .
METAL
TRASH

COPING WITH . . .
METAL TRASH

Jamie Daniel • Veronica Bonar
Illustrated by Tony Kenyon

Gareth Stevens Publishing
MILWAUKEE

For a free color catalog describing Gareth Stevens' list of high-quality books, call 1-800-341-3569 (USA) or 1-800-461-9120 (Canada).

Library of Congress Cataloging-in-Publication Data

Daniel, Jamie.
    Coping with— metal trash/adapted from Veronica Bonar's Metal rubbish! by Jamie
Daniel; illustrated by Tony Kenyon. — North American ed.
      p. cm. — (Trash busters)
    Includes bibliographical references and index.
    ISBN 0-8368-1058-9
    1. Metal wastes—Juvenile literature. 2. Refuse and refuse disposal—Juvenile literature.
[1. Metal wastes—Recycling. 2. Refuse and refuse disposal. 3. Recycling (Waste)] I.
Kenyon, Tony, ill. II. Bonar, Veronica. Metal rubbish! III. Title. IV. Series: Daniel, Jamie.
Trash busters.
TD799.5.D36   1994
363.72'82--dc20   93-32482

This North American edition first published in 1994 by

Gareth Stevens Publishing
1555 North RiverCenter Drive, Suite 201
Milwaukee, WI 53212, USA

This edition © 1994 by Zoë Books Limited. First produced as *METAL RUBBISH!,* © 1992 by Zoë Books Limited, original text © 1992 by Veronica Bonar. Additional end matter © 1994 by Gareth Stevens, Inc. Published in the USA by arrangement with Zoë Books Limited, Winchester, England. Published in Canada by arrangement with Heinemann Educational Books Ltd., Oxford, England.

Series editor: Patricia Lantier-Sampon
Cover design: Karen Knutson

Picture Credits:
Robert Harding Picture Library pp. 9, 12, 24; Oxford Scientific Films p. 15 (Ronald Toms); Scientific Photo Library p. 16 (Martin Bond), p. 21 (James Holmes, Coopers Metals), p. 26 (Alex Bartel); Zefa pp. 7, 11, 18, 22.

Printed in the USA

1 2 3 4 5 6 7 8 9 99 98 97 96 95 94

At this time, Gareth Stevens, Inc., does not use 100 percent recycled paper, although the paper used in our books does contain about 30 percent recycled fiber. This decision was made after a careful study of current recycling procedures revealed their dubious environmental benefits. We will continue to explore recycling options.

TABLE OF CONTENTS

Words that appear in the glossary are printed in **boldface** type the first time they occur in the text.

THE MANY USES OF METALS

We use metals every day. Our bicycles are made of metal, and so are our soda cans and the coins we use to pay for them. We cook food in metal pans and eat our meals with metal **silverware**. We sometimes wrap leftovers in metal **foil**.

The soft metal **copper** is used to make thin wire for telephone and electric power cables. Stronger metals like **iron** and **steel** are used to make cars, bridges, and ships. We can see metal products all around us.

⬆ These factory robots are helping build metal cars.

WHERE METALS COME FROM

Metals are found in the earth, usually in rock or soil. **Minerals** containing metals in rocks and soil are called **ores**. Long ago, people found that heating a certain type of dark red ore caused the metal inside to melt and leak out. This metal was iron.

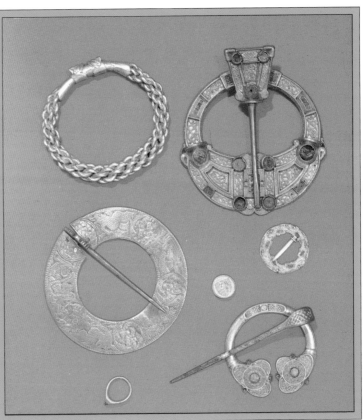

▲ People have used gold and silver for centuries to make jewelry.

Metals that are very rare are called **precious metals**. They are often used to make jewelry and are more costly than more common metals, such as iron and **aluminum**. Common metals are cheaper because they are easier to find and dig out of the ground.

USEFUL METALS

Some metals are more useful than others. One metal we use all the time is steel, which is a mixture of iron and **carbon**. Steel is used to support big buildings and to make cars, knives, and tools. Cans of food we buy at the supermarket are often made of steel and **tin**.

Aluminum is another useful metal. It is lighter and stronger than steel and does not rust. Airplanes, trains, soda cans, and toothpaste tubes are just a few products made from aluminum.

⬆ Aluminum is used to make helicopter parts because it is both light and strong.

11

METAL TRASH

⬆ Rusty metal trash ruins a sandy beach.

About one-sixth of everything we throw away is metal. Soft drink cans make up one percent of all our trash.

Metal trash should be disposed of carefully. A cut or scratch from rusty metal cans can be dangerous. As a result, a **germ** called **tetanus** can get into our bodies and make us sick.

When metal cans are tossed into trash cans, they will most likely be dumped into a **landfill**. The cans, with other trash, are then buried in the dirt. It is better to recycle metal objects than to throw them away.

Animals are often badly hurt by metal trash. They can cut themselves on sharp edges, become trapped in rusty cans, or get tangled in coils of rusty wire.

TRASH DUMPS ARE DANGEROUS

Unfortunately, a lot of metal trash is never taken to a landfill. Instead, people simply dump old metal on abandoned land. Such trash dumps are unsightly, and they also endanger people and animals.

This open trash area is ugly and dangerous.

Never play near an open trash area. Some metal trash contains dangerous or poisonous chemicals. These can leak out and make people and animals sick. Old cars, freezers, and refrigerators contain such dangerous chemicals.

15

METAL LITTER

Litter is trash that people carelessly throw on the ground or in other places. Since metal is often found in things like soda cans and tin foil, a lot of the litter left behind is made of metal. This litter pollutes the environment and makes the countryside unpleasant to look at.

◆ Littered drink cans make a mess!

Metal litter is not only ugly; it is also dangerous. Pop-top rings, for example, can cut people and kill animals that swallow them. After a picnic or an outing, always take your metal litter home, or throw it away in a public garbage can. Never leave litter of any kind lying around.

SORTING METAL TRASH

Some countries have laws that require people to sort their trash. Metal, plastic, glass, and paper trash are kept separate. This makes **recycling** trash easier. Metal trash is recycled by melting it down and then using it to make new metal products.

⬆ Old cars and metal pipes are carefully sorted for recycling.

Some people like to take advantage of the metal other people leave behind. Using **metal detectors**, they can find old coins, jewelry, or other useful metal objects in the ground.

METALS FOR SCRAP

Scrap dealers collect big items like old washing machines, machinery, and other metal waste. They profit by recycling these items.

Metal waste is put through a big machine called a **shredder**. The shredder breaks the metal into pieces. Iron and steel scrap metal are melted down to make new steel.

▲ A shredder breaks scrap metal into little pieces.

RECYCLING STEEL

▲ This huge magnet picks up steel trash.

Steel is easy to sort out from other trash. Huge **magnets** pick up steel objects and lift them out of the rest of the trash.

The used steel objects are then taken to factories to be recycled into new steel products. For example, every new steel can we use is made of about one-fourth recycled steel. Larger steel items, such as cars and storage tanks, can also be made of recycled steel.

ALUMINUM AND ENERGY

Every person in the modern world uses about 60 pounds (27 kilograms) of aluminum each year. Aluminum is made from an ore called **bauxite**. Making aluminum from bauxite consumes a lot of **energy**.

◆ Bauxite mining tears the land apart.

It makes sense to recycle aluminum because recycling consumes much less energy than making new aluminum. Also, aluminum does not get weaker as it is recycled, as do some other metals. Many soda cans are now made from recycled aluminum.

RECYCLING ALUMINUM

It is important to sort aluminum cans from other trash. Magnets cannot pick up aluminum, and it often gets buried in landfills when it could be recycled.

To see if a can is made of aluminum, put a magnet up to its side. If the magnet does not stick, the can is made of aluminum.

◆ These aluminum cans have been squashed together and are now ready to be recycled.

To help recycle aluminum, save soda cans and anything else that is made of aluminum, such as food containers and foil. Wash the cans and other items well, and squash them so they take up less space. Then recycle them through a program in your town or city. Your efforts to recycle will help preserve the environment and keep it beautiful.

GLOSSARY

aluminum: a lightweight silver metal used to make cookware, airplanes, and many other things.

bauxite: an ore needed to make aluminum.

carbon: a non-metal element found in many forms, including coal and diamonds.

copper: a soft, reddish brown metal that is especially good for conducting electricity and heat.

energy: the power necessary to do any sort of work. We eat food to get the energy we need for our bodies, and machines make energy to perform tasks from different types of fuel.

foil: a very thin sheet of metal. Foil can be bent like paper to wrap

things but, unlike paper, it will not burn.

germ: a tiny organism that can cause disease.

iron: a hard, gray metal used in making many tools and machines.

landfill: a big hole in the ground where trash is dumped and then covered with soil.

litter: the trash people carelessly throw on the ground or in other places, such as lakes or streams.

magnets: metal bars that attract iron or steel. Magnets can be used to lift iron and steel from trash dumps so they can be recycled.

metal detectors: small machines that detect buried or hidden metal.

They make a beeping sound when they detect metal.

minerals: inorganic (non-living) substances or elements found in nature, such as coal, ore, and salt, that are mined for human use.

ore: a mineral or minerals from which metals can be mined.

precious metals: rare metals that are considered very valuable. Gold and silver are precious metals.

recycling: the process of making a new product from an old product that has already been used. Many metal, glass, plastic, and paper products can be recycled.

scrap: leftover pieces or fragments; something that is thrown away because it is no longer useful.

shredder: a machine that cuts objects into small pieces or shreds.

silverware: eating utensils made of or coated with silver or some other shiny metal.

steel: a strong, hard metal made by melting iron together with other ingredients.

tetanus: a disease that can enter a person's body through a cut made by rusty metal. Tetanus causes muscles in the body to become paralyzed.

tin: a soft, shiny metal that does not rust easily. Tin is often used as an outer coating on other metals.

PLACES TO WRITE

Here are some places you can write for more information about metal trash and how it can be recycled. Be sure to include your name and address, and be clear about what information you would like to know. Include a self-addressed, stamped envelope for a reply.

Greenpeace Foundation
185 Spadina Avenue
Sixth Floor
Toronto, Ontario
M5T 2C6

The National Recycling
   Coalition
1101 30th Street NW
Suite 305
Washington, D.C. 20007

Institute of Scrap
   Recycling Industries
1325 G Street NW
Suite 1000
Washington, D.C. 20005

INTERESTING FACTS ABOUT METAL

Did you know . . .

▸ that most metal cans are made of about one-fourth recycled metal?

▸ that many huge jet airplanes are made of lightweight aluminum, the same metal used to make soft drink cans?

▸ that gold and silver jewelry made thousands of years ago has been found by researchers, still as beautiful as when it was made?

▸ that traces of silver are needed to make black-and-white photographs?

▸ that playing in a trash dump isn't just smelly — it's also dangerous? Dumps are full of broken glass and sharp pieces of metal. Never play in a dump.

MORE BOOKS TO READ

Iron and Steel. M. Lambert (Rourke Corporation)

Metals and Alloys. Kathryn Whyman (Franklin Watts)

Metals: Born of Earth and Fire. Jean-Pierre Reymond (Young Discovery Library)

Reducing, Reusing, and Recycling. Bobby Kalman (Crabtree)

What We Can Do About Protecting Nature. Donna Bailey (Watts)

Where Does Garbage Go? Isaac Asimov (Gareth Stevens)

INDEX